This book belongs to

Hide and Seek
Find whimsy & wonder within

Hiding in these pages are old friends and new stories.
Whether you like masked balls, secret gardens, or hidden treasures
you will find what you seek inside.
All illustrations are hand-drawn by R.J. Hampson.

Uncover charming and irresistible scenes
in this delightful coloring book.
For coloring enthusiasts and explorers of all ages!

See more at rjhampson.com

Published by Hop Skip Jump. PO Box 1324 Buderim Queensland Australia 4556
First published 2024. Copyright © 2024 R.J. Hampson.

All Rights Reserved. Without limiting the rights under copyright reserved above, no part of this publication may be reproduced, stored in or introduced into a retrieval system, or transmitted, in any form or by any means (electronic, mechanical, photocopying, recording or otherwise), without the prior written permission of both the copyright owner and the above publisher of this book. The only exception is by a reviewer who may share short excerpts in a review.

ISBN: 978-1-922472-39-7

hopskipjump®

Using this book

Find a quiet place away from distractions. Relax and immerse yourself in the process of coloring as you explore the details of each illustration.

Experiment! There are no correct color choices. Try different color palettes or mediums and get inspiration from other colorists.

This book is best suited to color pencils or markers. Wet mediums should be used sparingly. Slide a card or sheets of paper behind the illustration you are coloring to avoid marker bleed through.

Find fresh coloring pages by signing up to Russell's newsletter. Get free downloadable pages and updates on new books at -
rjhampson.com

THE ELEPHANT IN THE ROOM

DEEP IN THE WOODS

INVISIBILITY POTION

A CAMOUFLAGE OF CHAMELEONS

OPPORTUNITY KNOCKS

CURIOSITY

MASKED BALL

SPECIAL DELIVERY

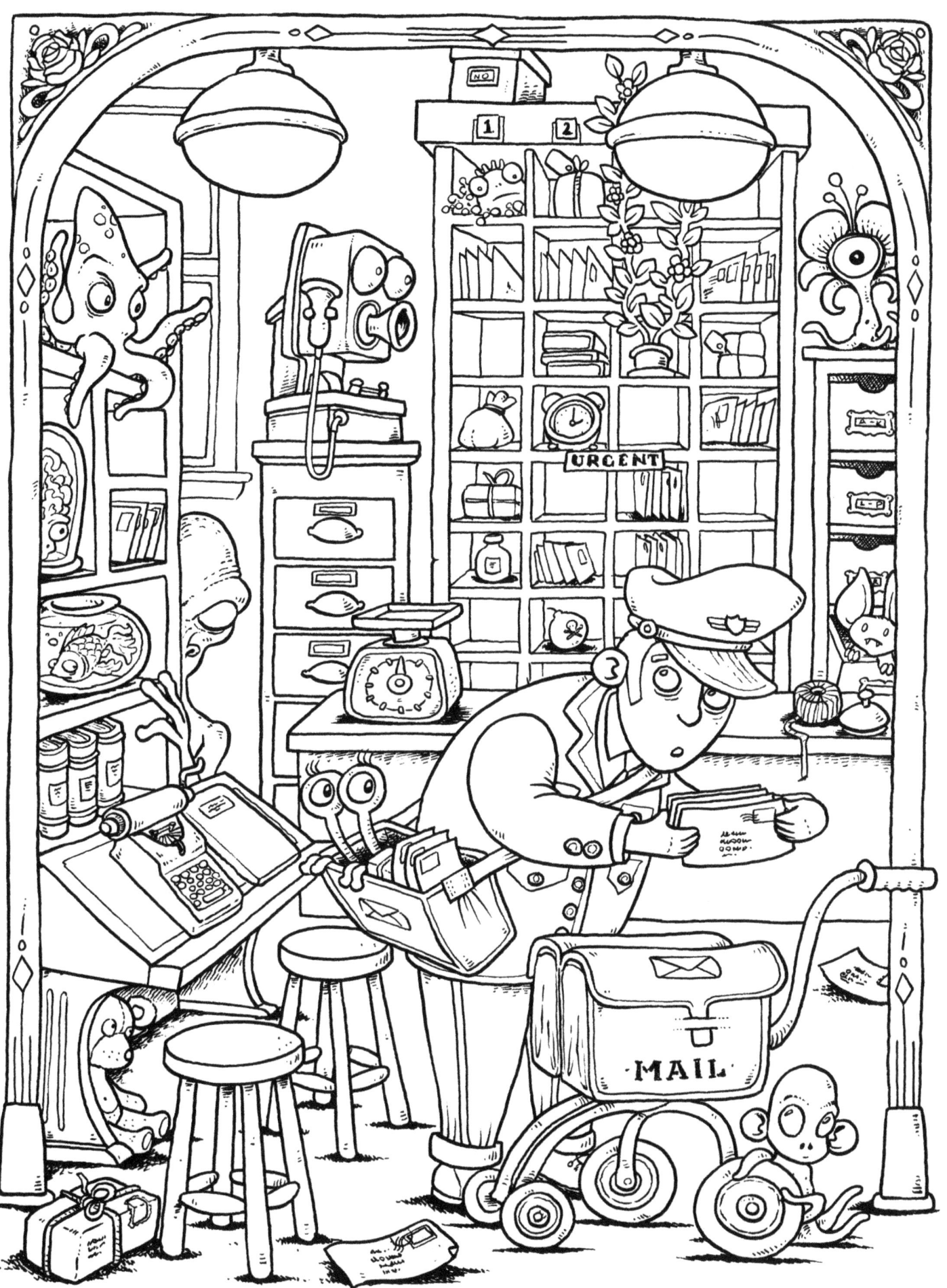

SECRET SANCTUARY

CAMPFIRE TALES:
THE RETURN OF THE BUG CATCHER

HIDETH AND SEEKETH

THE SECRET GARDEN

PREPARING FOR THE HUNT

TREASURES IN THE DEEP

AUSSIE SUMMER

MUSHROOM MAYHEM

TAKE ME TO YOUR LEADER!

MR FOGHERTY INVESTIGATES

DRAGON VASE

DASTARDLY DECORATIONS

THE PLANT COLLECTOR

WRAPPING UP CHRISTMAS

LUNCHTIME

PEEK-A-BOO

Don't let the music stop!

Find new coloring pages by signing up to R.J. Hampson's newsletter.
Get free downloadable pages, monthly coloring sheets,
and updates on new books at -
rjhampson.com/coloring

Thanks for choosing this coloring book.
If you enjoyed it, please consider leaving a review.
It will help to let more people in on the experience
plus you'd certainly make this illustrator very happy!

More books in this series

 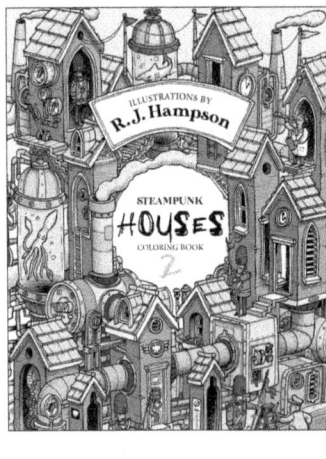  
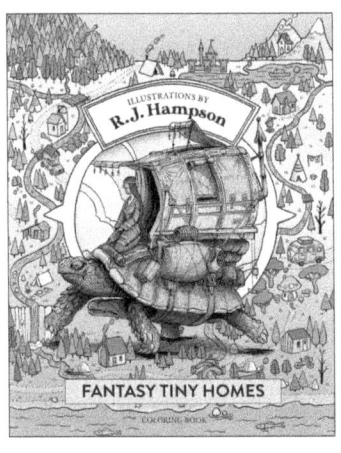 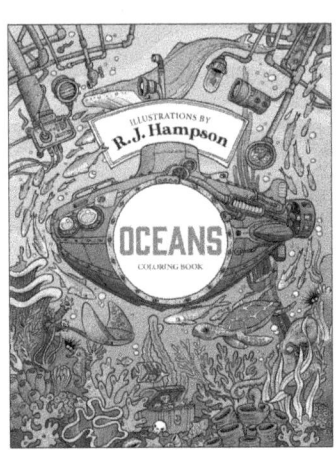  
  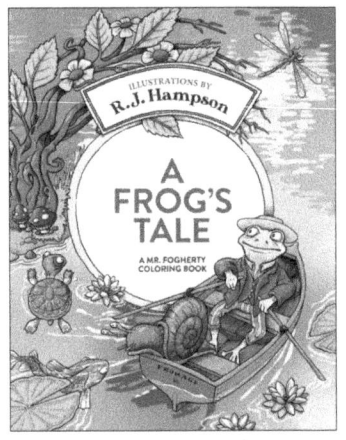 

See flip-throughs for all coloring books at **rjhampson.com**

www.ingramcontent.com/pod-product-compliance
Lightning Source LLC
Chambersburg PA
CBHW041221240426
43661CB00012B/1106